WHAT TO LOOK FOR
at the
CATHEDRAL

Philip Sauvain

D1823147

Contents

HOW A CATHEDRAL DIFFERS FROM A CHURCH

Do you know why a cathedral is different from an ordinary church? It is not just that a cathedral is usually much bigger than a parish church.

The bishop's mitre

If you look carefully in a cathedral you will probably be able to find a statue or a picture in a stained glass window showing a bishop.

You will also see a small picture of his mitre somewhere in the cathedral – on a memorial perhaps or on a coat of arms. The mitre is the very special headdress worn by a bishop. When you see it you know that the person wearing it is a bishop.

Can you see a mitre in the picture on these pages?

Cathedrals a long time ago

Most British cathedrals are several hundred years old. Some were built soon after the Norman Conquest about eight to nine hundred years ago.

Picturing the past

When you visit a great cathedral try to picture what it was like hundreds of years ago when it was first built.

Think of the workers who risked their lives to build the tower or the spire. You can see a picture of medieval building workers like these on pages 6–7.

Try to think what the cathedral was like inside when candles were the only source of light when it was dark.

Picture the monks, priests and the bishop in his mitre walking in procession down the aisles. Can you imagine what it was like to hear the chanting of the monks?

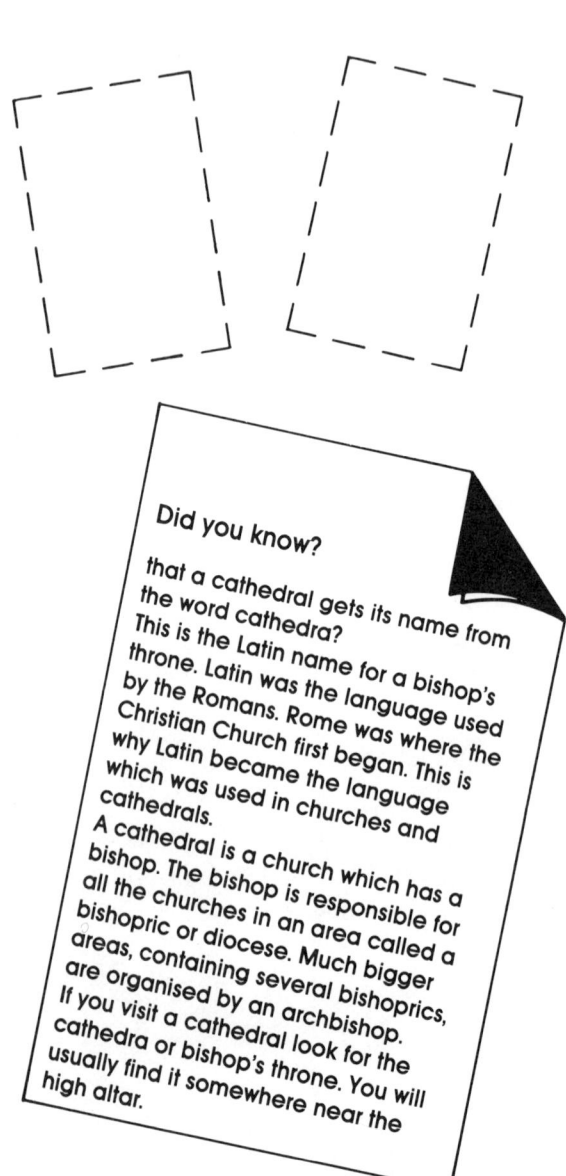

Did you know?

that a cathedral gets its name from the word cathedra? This is the Latin name for a bishop's throne. Latin was the language used by the Romans. Rome was where the Christian Church first began. This is why Latin became the language which was used in churches and cathedrals.

A cathedral is a church which has a bishop. The bishop is responsible for all the churches in an area called a bishopric or diocese. Much bigger areas, containing several bishoprics, are organised by an archbishop. If you visit a cathedral look for the cathedra or bishop's throne. You will usually find it somewhere near the high altar.

The precinct

Many cathedrals have a special area close to the cathedral called the precinct. Have any of the cathedrals you have visited got a precinct?

In some cathedrals, like Norwich and Canterbury, you can enter the precinct through a medieval archway. This is because a wall surrounds part of the precinct.

In other cathedrals the precinct may be a large square, or even a lawn, surrounded by houses belonging to the Church.

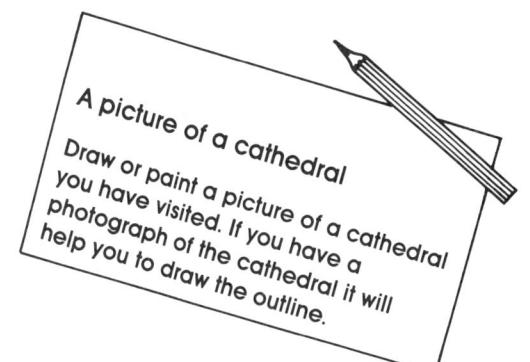

A picture of a cathedral

Draw or paint a picture of a cathedral you have visited. If you have a photograph of the cathedral it will help you to draw the outline.

HOW CATHEDRALS DIFFER

How many towers and spires are there in the cathedrals you have seen in pictures or on a visit?

Towers and spires
Part of the pleasure you can get from visiting cathedrals is seeing how each one is different. Many have splendid spires and towers.

Repairs
The oldest cathedrals you are likely to see are those started by the Normans. It took many years to build them and most were altered a lot in the eight or nine hundred years since they were first begun.

Stonework crumbled, arches collapsed, parts of the cathedral were damaged by fire. The cathedral had to be repaired and made new again. Wealthy people gave money to the Church, so that new extensions could be added to the cathedral to make it larger.

Alterations
This is why a Norman cathedral may have Norman windows and doorways with round arches. But it probably has other features as well which were added later on, such as a spire built four hundred years ago.

At each of the different periods in the past, church builders had different ways of doing things. It was rather like the way in which styles of cars and fashions in clothes change nowadays from year to year.

Different styles
Sometimes the changes were because builders found better or safer ways of doing things. Sometimes, like changes to clothes, it was because they liked the look of the new styles more than the old.

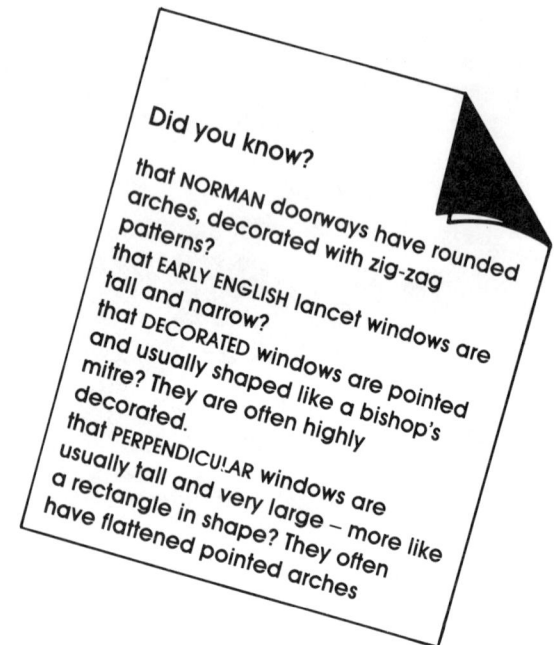

Did you know?

that NORMAN doorways have rounded arches, decorated with zig-zag patterns?

that EARLY ENGLISH lancet windows are tall and narrow?

that DECORATED windows are pointed and usually shaped like a bishop's mitre? They are often highly decorated.

that PERPENDICULAR windows are usually tall and very large – more like a rectangle in shape? They often have flattened pointed arches

Gothic arches

The Normans (800–900 years ago) built thick walls and small windows because they did not know how to support high buildings in any other way. Even then their towers sometimes fell down! Later church builders discovered how to support the walls and make them much stronger. As a result much larger windows could be built into the walls to let more light into the cathedral. These windows usually have Gothic arches. This is the name given to arches which come to a point at the top.

Styles of building

In Britain the main styles of building to be seen in churches and cathedrals are called:

NORMAN (built about 800–900 years ago),
EARLY ENGLISH (built about 700–800 years ago),
DECORATED (built about 600–700 years ago),
PERPENDICULAR (built about 450–600 years ago).

Perpendicular windows are often seen in cathedrals. At the time when they were first built there were many rich merchants in Britain. The merchants gave money to build new churches and cathedrals.

Have you seen a Perpendicular window in a cathedral or in a local church?

Making a set of medieval cathedral windows

Look closely at the shapes of the four main types of medieval cathedral window – NORMAN – EARLY ENGLISH – DECORATED – PERPENDICULAR. Use soft modelling clay to make a model of each window.

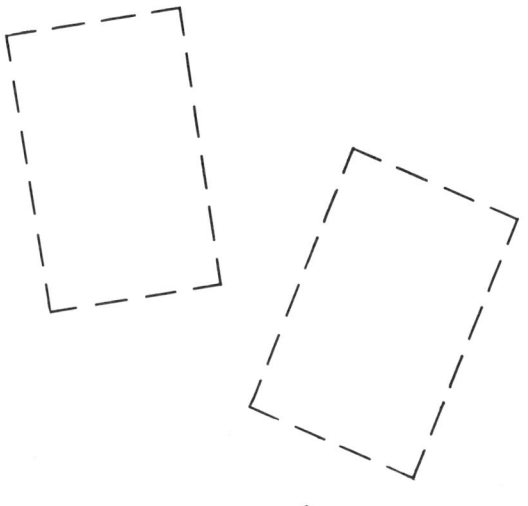

BUILDING A CATHEDRAL

Can you imagine what it must have been like to build a great cathedral hundreds of years ago in the Middle Ages?

Tools

There were none of the modern machines and giant cranes you can see on a building site today.

Even so, you would probably be able to recognise many of the tools the stonemasons and carpenters used. They had saws, chisels, hammers, mallets and nails.

Stone

Most cathedrals were built of stone. This had to be cut to shape and fitted so that it matched the rest of the building. The cathedral builders needed stone which was soft enough to be cut and carved, yet hard enough to last a long time.

This is why stone was often brought to the site of the cathedral from stone quarries a long way away – such as Caen in northern France. It was carried by barge along the coast or up a river and delivered to the site on a cart.

Workmen

Workmen dragged the stones to where they were needed on wooden sleds (a sledge on dry land) or wheeled them in simple wheelbarrows.

It was heavy back-breaking work – especially when the blocks of stone had to be carried to the top of a cathedral tower. Sometimes they were pulled up a long wooden ramp (like a slide at a children's playground).

Other workmen prepared the mortar (a type of cement), When it set hard it stuck (bonded) a stone to the other stones in the wall.

Scaffolding

Cathedral towers are very high. This is why the stonemasons needed wooden scaffolding so they could work in safety. This was very similar to the steel scaffolding you can see today. Can you see the scaffolding on the cathedral building site in the picture?

Did you know?

that most medieval churches and cathedrals were planned by a master mason?
We would call him an architect today. Mason is the name given to anyone who works with stone (or masonry). Some stonemasons were skilled at carving stone into shape. They used a stone chisel to make faces and patterns. You can see their designs and their gargoyles in cathedrals today. Other stonemasons, called freemasons, worked with softer stone which could be cut into shape to fit round archways and doors.

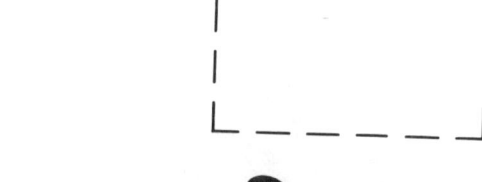

Make a model of a cathedral

Make a tiny model of a cathedral out of soft modelling clay. Most cathedrals are shaped like a cross, so you should find it easy to get the main shape of the cathedral right. Use the pictures in this book to help you.

The foundations

The workmen had to lay solid foundations many metres deep. This was to stop the heavy stone cathedral sinking into the ground. Large numbers of workers with shovels and picks were needed as well as hundreds of cartloads of stone and rubble.

The walls

The walls of the cathedral had to be strong enough to support the weight of the roof. Windows only made them weaker. The Normans built very thick walls, thinking this was the best way to make them strong. But even this was not always successful and sometimes the roofs collapsed.

Buttresses

This is why strong pillars of stone were built against the walls to stop the walls falling over. These pillars are called buttresses and you can often see them supporting the walls of medieval churches and cathedrals.

About 750 years ago, masons began to build flying buttresses. These were very strong stone pillars built close to the cathedral walls and connected to them by arches. This is why they are called flying buttresses.

Flying buttresses made it possible to build walls that were thinner and stronger. The invention of Gothic arches which came to a point also made it possible to build larger windows without weakening the walls. They made the inside of a cathedral much lighter.

ENTERING THE CATHEDRAL

Cathedrals and churches have many things in common.

Features to look for
All have a nave. This is a place where the people can stand or sit during the service. There is usually a pulpit for the priest when giving the sermon, a lectern for the bible, an organ, choirstalls for the people in the choir and a high altar. When you enter the cathedral see if you can find these features. But before you go in look carefully at the entrance.

Sanctuary knockers
Sanctuary door knockers can still be seen today, like the one at Durham Cathedral on the colour stamp.

When you enter a cathedral take a close look at the door and the doorway. Does it have a special door knocker? How thick is the door? Does the arch look anything like the archways shown in the pictures on pages 4–5?

East and west; north and south
In most cathedrals the main entrance is either through the west door or the south porch. Most cathedrals have been built so that the altar is at the eastern end of the church. See if you can find out why they did this.

The south porch was often used as a meeting place in the Middle Ages. Traders carried out business deals here and at one time part of the marriage service was conducted in the porch rather than in the cathedral.

Shaped like a cross
Cathedrals almost always have a layout like the one shown here. As you can see it is shaped like a cross. The upper part of the cross is where the choir, high altar and an area called the presbytery are found. The lower part of the cross is the nave. The two arms of the cross are called the transepts. Because the altar is in the east, the transepts face north and south.

Did you know?

that in the Middle Ages, a thief or a murderer was safe from punishment in a church or cathedral?

It was called seeking sanctuary. This is a word meaning a place of safety. The church or cathedral was a holy place, so soldiers were not allowed to come in to seize someone wanted by the king.

Imagine the scene in the Middle Ages as a thief is chased through the narrow streets of a city. Despite the cries of "Stop Thief!" she escapes being caught by the people who have joined in the hue and cry. She reaches the cathedral panting and puffing and bangs hard on the sanctuary door knocker to get into the cathedral. Once inside she is safe from arrest. No one dare follow her inside.

But she can only stay there for forty days and can only escape capture if she promises to leave England for good.

A plan of a cathedral

Draw or trace a plan of a cathedral. You can usually buy a guide with a plan of the cathedral which you can copy.
Alternatively, draw a large cross on a sheet of paper and then add bits to it as you walk round the cathedral. You could mark in where the main entrances are, where the transepts and the side chapels are situated. Show where the huge columns stand which support the roof of the nave. Mark in and name the nave, the choir and the high altar.

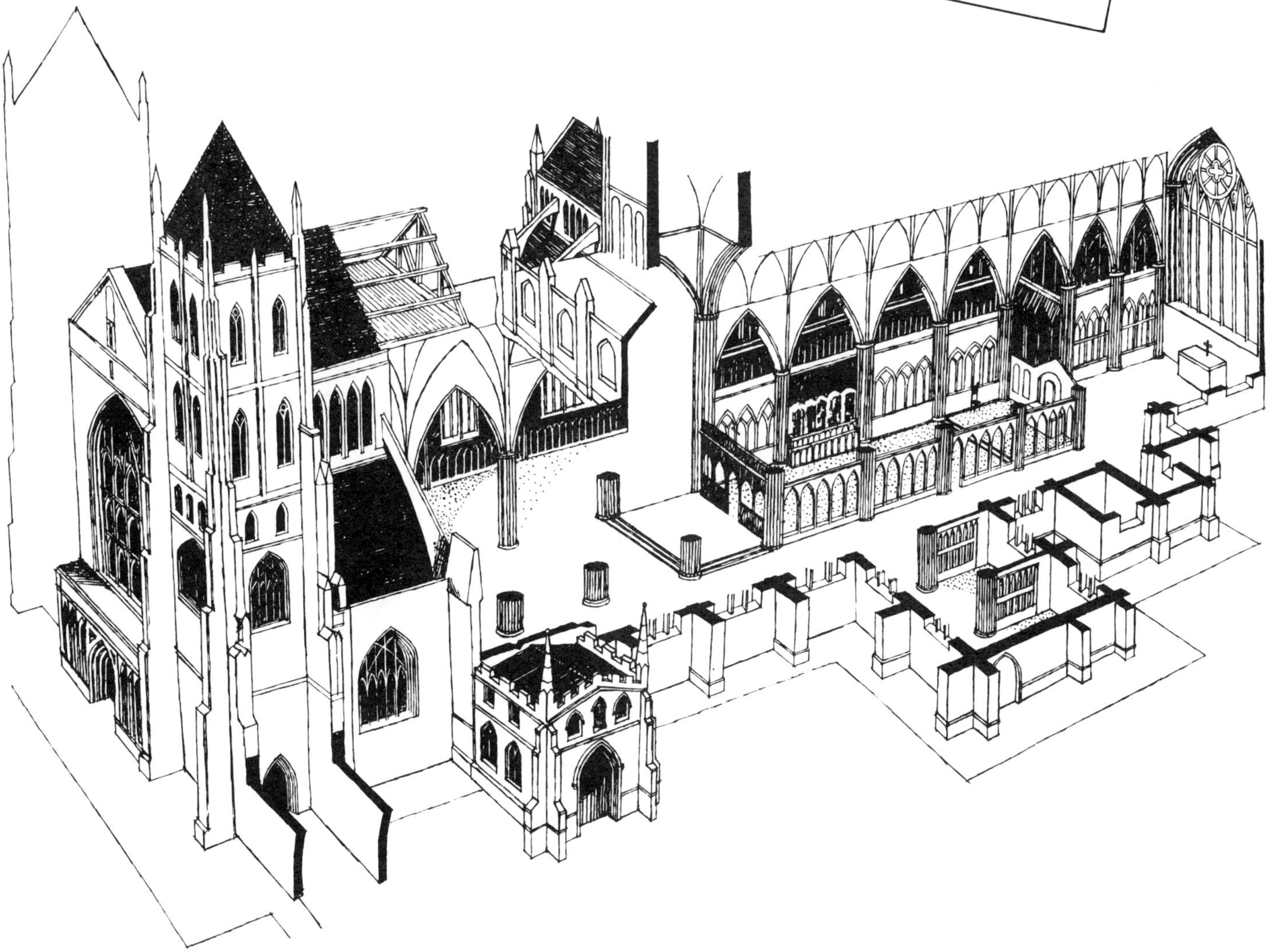

THE PEOPLE'S CHURCH

In the Middle Ages many churches only had pews (seats) for well-to-do people. It was usually standing room only in the nave for the ordinary person!

This is why the floor was often covered with straw. People brought mud on their boots into the nave. You could even take your dog into church with you!

The services

Ordinary people in the Middle Ages could neither read nor write. In any case there were no prayer or hymn books. Printing came to Britain a long time after the building of the first cathedrals.

Instead priests used wall pictures to tell the people stories from the bible. About 350 years ago, many of these wall paintings and statues were destroyed by Puritans. They thought there should be no pictures in a church. Stained glass windows help us to remember the days when paintings decorated the walls of British cathedrals and churches.

Stained glass windows

Much of the stained glass you can see in a cathedral is fairly new. But you may be lucky enough to visit a cathedral, like York Minster or Canterbury Cathedral, where there are still many colourful and interesting stained glass windows from the Middle Ages.

If you look carefully you may be able to pick out some of the stories from the bible.

Stained glass windows which were put up in memory of wealthy local people, such as a knight and his wife, can also help to tell you about the clothes people wore in the past.

In some stained glass windows you can see medieval castles and ships; kings and queens; birds and dogs; farmers and gardeners; horses, chickens and sheep; sailors and soldiers; thieves, knights and ladies.

The roof

When you stand in the nave look upwards at the roof. Notice the huge columns which support it.

How do you think workmen were able to put into position the carvings and other stonework you can see high above you?

The design of the roof was very important. Stone arches were built to support the roof timbers above. These stone ribs were often carved in graceful designs.

Where the stone arches crossed each other the stonemasons sometimes put a roof boss, so you could not see the join. The roof boss was a carved stone. Sometimes it had a design on it – such as a bunch of flowers. In some cathedrals the roof bosses show scenes from everyday life, such as windmills, packhorses and churches.

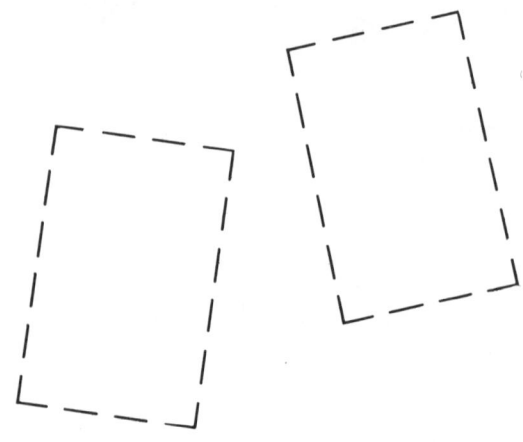

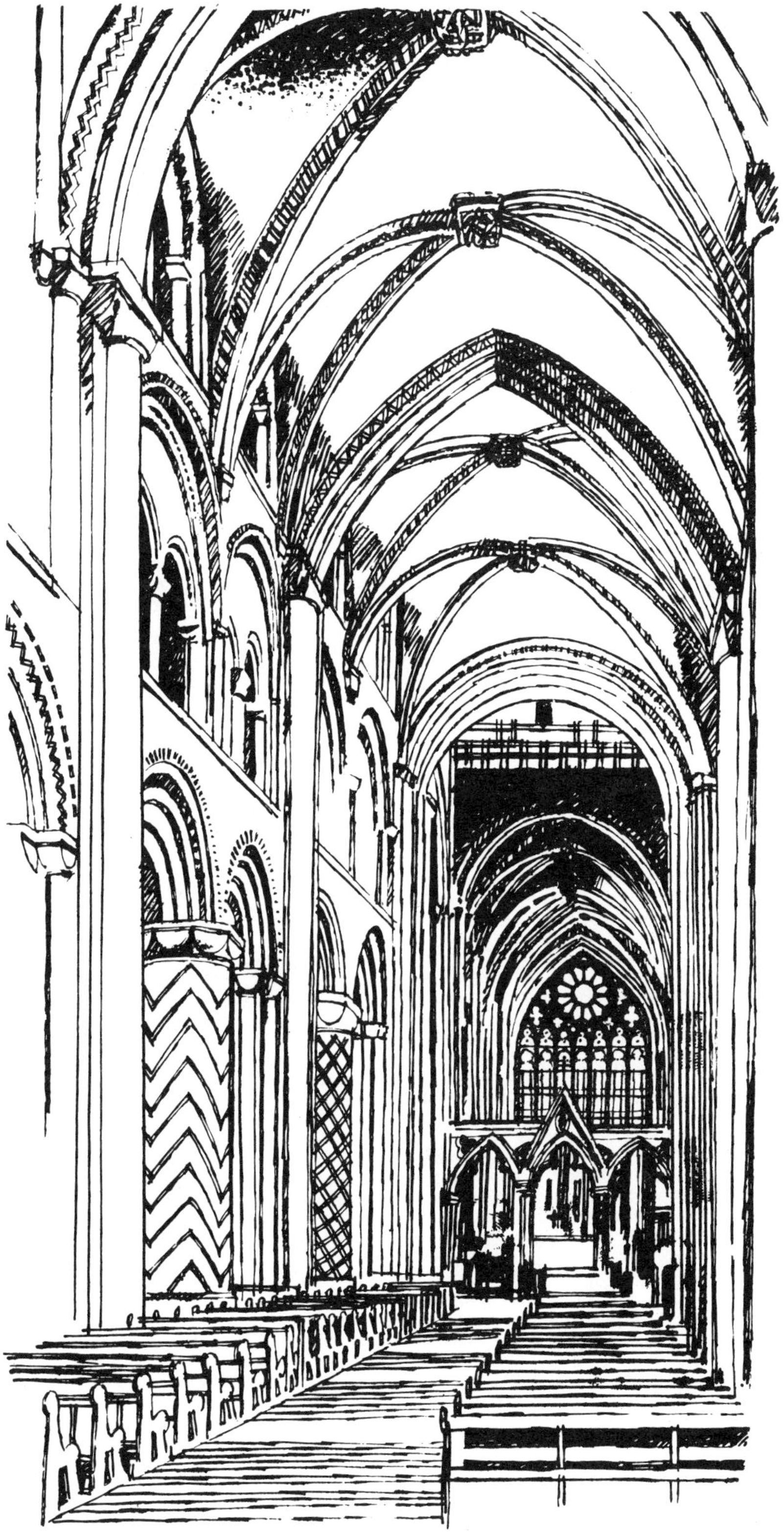

Did you know?

that medieval stained glass windows showing scenes from the bible often tell you something about everyday life in the Middle Ages? This is because the makers of the stained glass knew very little history. They did not know what life was really like in Palestine 2,000 years ago. They assumed that the people in the bible stories wore similar clothes to their own. So they showed Roman soldiers carrying medieval weapons and wearing medieval armour! Shepherds are dressed in the warm clothes needed for Britain's cold and damp weather rather than for the hot and sunny lands of Palestine!

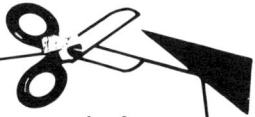

Make your own stained glass window

Stained glass makes a colourful picture because light shines through the glass. If you paint a picture on tracing paper and hold it up to the light you can make it look like stained glass.

1 Trace the shape of a church window.
2 On it draw a picture of a scene from the bible.
3 Divide your picture into small sections with black lines. These show the strips of lead which hold the pieces of stained glass together in a real church window.
4 Use bright colours to colour in the different parts of your picture.
5 Make the picture look like stained glass by placing it against a window.

THE CHOIR OF THE CATHEDRAL

When you walk to the end of the nave you will probably reach the transepts of the cathedral – the short arm of the cross at the centre of the church.

The choir
Between the transepts and the high altar you can see the choir. Beyond it is the sanctuary or presbytery. The choir is sometimes screened off from the nave since this is the part of the cathedral which was used by monks and priests and where special services are held today.

Services
The organ and choir-stalls are situated in the choir. The choir-stalls were where the priests and monks sat.

Services in the past were sung not spoken. In the Middle Ages they often went on a long time and for much of that time the clergy had to remain standing.

This was hard on the old and feeble. So the seats were cleverly designed so that they tipped up. Underneath the seat was a ledge where the clergyman could rest his weight during a long service – even though he appeared to be standing!

The seat took pity on him! Since the Latin word for pity is misericordia these tip-up seats were called misericorde seats.

Misericorde seats
The craftsmen who carved the choir stalls used their skill to cut interesting designs underneath the misericorde seats. These often show scenes of everyday life.

Be sure to ask for special permission if you want to look at the choir stalls and the misericorde seats. A guide will probably show them to you. They have old carvings and are priceless treasures. They could easily be damaged if the seats were allowed to slam down.

Did you know?

that some misericorde seats, such as those in Worcester Cathedral, show farmers harvesting corn?
At Exeter a carving of a strong man has been made so cleverly that he looks as if he is holding up the misericorde seat above him! At Ely Cathedral a demon listens to the conversation between two monks! Many show animals and birds, such as foxes in Bristol Cathedral, a deer and a snake in Ely Cathedral and an owl in Norwich Cathedral.
In the parish church at Fairford in Gloucestershire a carving shows a woman spinning wool whilst her dog dips his head in the bowl of stew in front of her! A carving in Bristol Cathedral shows a man and a woman quarrelling over a cauldron of meat!

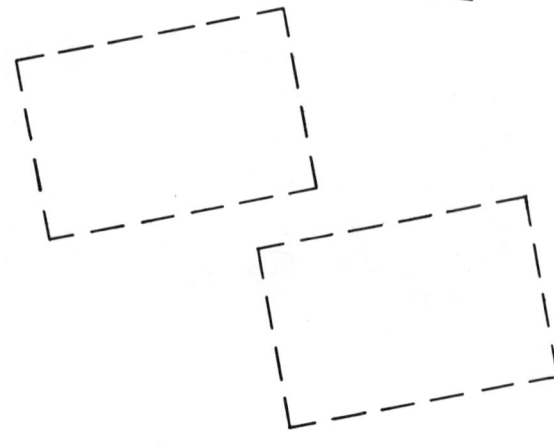

Bench ends

Carvings are also to be found on the ends of choir-stalls or the wooden pews in the nave. These are called bench ends.

About 400 years ago many pews were put in the nave for ordinary people to sit on. The woodcarvers often used their skill to carve scenes from everyday life on these bench ends as well as on the misericorde seats in the choir.

Everyday life in Tudor times

At Bishops Lydeard Church in Somerset you can see a splendid windmill on one bench end. It was carved at about the time when Henry VIII was King of England. Another bench end shows a medieval ship.

At Altarnun Church in Cornwall carvings on bench ends which were made at about the same time show musicians playing the bagpipes and a violin. Another carving shows a jester in cap and bells. Jesters were the comedians of the Middle Ages.

See if you can find any wooden carvings in the next church or cathedral you visit.

Sedilia

You may also see three stone seats set in the south wall of the sanctuary, near the high altar. These were used by the priest and his assistants during High Mass. They are called sedilia after the Latin word for seat.

A modern misericorde seat

What do you think a medieval woodcarver would carve today on the back of a church seat? What could show people in five hundred years time about life in your town or village today? Use pencil and paper to design two or three modern misericorde seats like those shown in the pictures.

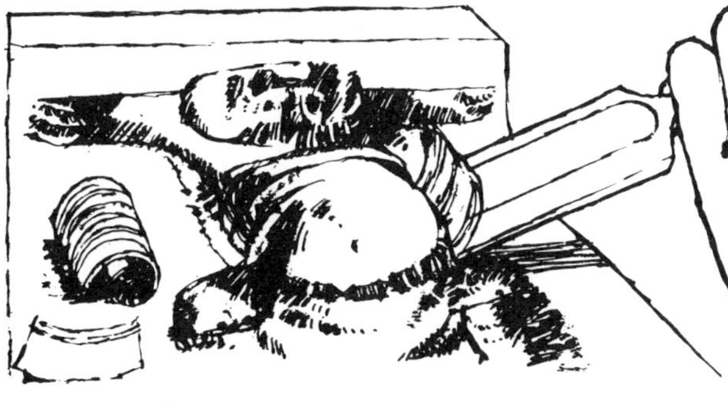

REMEMBERING THE DEAD

Sometimes the last resting place of an important person was marked by an effigy in the cathedral. This is a statue of a person at rest.

Effigies

Effigies of bishops and nobles can be seen in many cathedrals. From them you can find out about clothes in the past.

In some cathedrals you can see an effigy of a knight in full armour, sometimes resting by the side of his wife. Effigies like these can help you to see what armour was worn at the time and how women were dressed.

Memorials

Most of the memorials in the cathedral are no more than about three hundred years old. Some commemorate men who died in wars and battles long ago. Some tell you about trades and businesses of the past.

If you look at the ages when people died you can see that they usually died younger than people do now.

Many memorials tell you where people lived or worked. If you look long enough you will probably find monuments to people who worked in what was then the British Empire – in America, Africa and Australia.

Many cathedrals have memorials to famous people although most are in St. Paul's Cathedral and Westminster Abbey.

If you look hard you may see monuments and memorials to heroes and heroines of the past. For instance you can see monuments to St. Thomas Becket and the Black Prince in Canterbury Cathedral and the First World War heroine Edith Cavell in Norwich Cathedral.

Brasses

Brasses are another interesting memorial to look out for. These have designs which were etched on a sheet of brass. Memorial brasses often show knights in armour and ladies in the splendid fashions of the past.

Make a brass rubbing

Use this method to make a rubbing of a coin. Place paper over the coin holding it tightly so it will not slip. Use a crayon or a soft pencil to rub gently over the surface of the paper. An image of the coin will appear like magic on the paper.
This is a good way to make a picture of a collection of foreign coins.
Make rubbings of other raised surfaces, such as the bark from a tree or an unwanted gramophone record.

The picture on a brass may be difficult to pick out. It usually stands out best if you look at it from an angle or when the sun shines on it.

Brass rubbings

There is an even better way of looking at the picture on the brass. This is by making a brass rubbing.

Because the picture is cut into the brass sheet it stands out like the picture of the Queen on a coin. By placing paper over the brass and rubbing smoothly with a piece of cobbler's wax, an expert brass rubber can make a perfect copy of the picture on the brass.

It stands out in white (where there are cuts in the brass) whilst the rest of the picture is black (where the brass has a smooth unmarked surface).

Did you know?

that in one brass in St. Margaret's Church in King's Lynn in Norfolk you can see a great feast in progress? The main dish served at the banquet was peacock! From this brass you can get a splendid idea of what a banquet was like in the Middle Ages.

EVERYDAY LIFE IN A CATHEDRAL

You can find out a lot about everyday life in the past when you walk round a great cathedral.

Stone carvings

On the walls of Lincoln Cathedral stone carvings of biblical scenes show boats and also medieval peasants working in the fields.

Sometimes you can even see what the craftsmen who built the cathedral looked like. The carvings they made of people from the bible were sometimes a good likeness of themselves or of their friends, the clergy and their fellow craftsmen.

This was an old tradition which can be seen in modern cathedrals today as well as in those built hundreds of years ago. Nowadays the stonemason will probably use an electric drill to make the carving rather than a chisel and a hammer!

Gargoyles

Even a gargoyle (like the one shown on the colour stamp) may have been a likeness of one of the masons or of someone the craftsman particularly disliked in the cathedral or in the city!

Gargoyles were water spouts, draining water from the cathedral roof.

Rather than have the end of the spout spoiling the effect of their work, stonemasons carved a face there – the open mouth being the place where the water could run out!

Visiting a cathedral today

See if you can find carvings in stone in the cathedral showing scenes from everyday life or ordinary people.

Places to look for include the gargoyles at the edge of a roof and the decorations high up on the walls of the cathedral.

Coats of arms

Look carefully at any monument to a bishop, lord and lady, or knight. You will probably find a shield on it somewhere – with a coat of arms like the one in the colour stamp.

Once you start looking for coats of arms you will be surprised at the number you can usually find in a cathedral.

Did you know?

that most cathedrals have special treasures, such as famous paintings, rare books and old tapestries? These are not always on show because they are fragile and often very valuable.

Lincoln Cathedral has a copy of Magna Carta, the Great Charter of freedom which King John had to accept in 1215.

Hereford Cathedral has a library of chained books. They contain many illuminated manuscripts and were chained to the bookshelves to stop people taking them away.

Hereford also has one of the oldest maps in Britain. It is a map of the world (called the Mappa Mundi) which was drawn about seven hundred years ago on fine parchment.

Making a gargoyle

You may not think of yourself as being good at art but you can probably make a small gargoyle out of soft modelling clay. Gargoyles are interesting sculptures but they are not usually attractive to look at! So whatever you make in modelling clay need not be lifelike or realistic or beautiful!

Remember that the back of the gargoyle is hollow and that water gushed out – usually through the mouth.

THE CATHEDRAL IN PEOPLE'S LIVES

People in the Middle Ages used the cathedral much more than most townspeople do today. It was the centre of their everyday life.

Many people went to services every day; not just on Sundays. The Church, then as now, looked after people throughout their lives. They were baptised into the Christian Church at its font, married before its altar and buried in its graveyard.

The font
Look for the font when you visit a cathedral. Some cathedrals have fonts with great canopies above them. Others are simple stone bowls, many of them with carvings round the sides.

In some churches and cathedrals these carvings also show scenes from everyday life, such as the font at Brookland Parish Church in Kent which shows a year's farming activities.

The cathedral school
When the children grew older some of the boys went to the cathedral school. This was often run by the monks who worked in the cathedral.

Many cathedrals still have a school attached to them. Some only teach the boys who sing in the choir. Others are famous public schools, like King's School, Canterbury.

Mystery plays
In the Middle Ages people looked forward to the annual mystery or miracle plays. They were first performed by priests and choirboys in the church or cathedral itself to tell stories from the bible. Later when they became very popular they were performed out of doors – at first in the churchyard and later in the streets of the medieval city. By this time they were usually performed by guilds of craftsmen – such as the carpenters and the fishmongers. These mystery plays were often very funny as well as being serious plays about stories such as Noah's Ark.

Cathedral priories

Although we think of abbeys and priories as being different from cathedrals, they were closely linked in the past. In fact some cathedrals were originally abbey churches and only made into cathedrals at a much later date.

Other cathedrals were built from the start with a priory attached. The monks took an active part in the life of the cathedral. They helped to run the cathedral's school and trained its choir.

When you visit a cathedral see if it had a priory attached to it in the past.

Look for the cloisters and the chapter house where the monks met each day to do business.

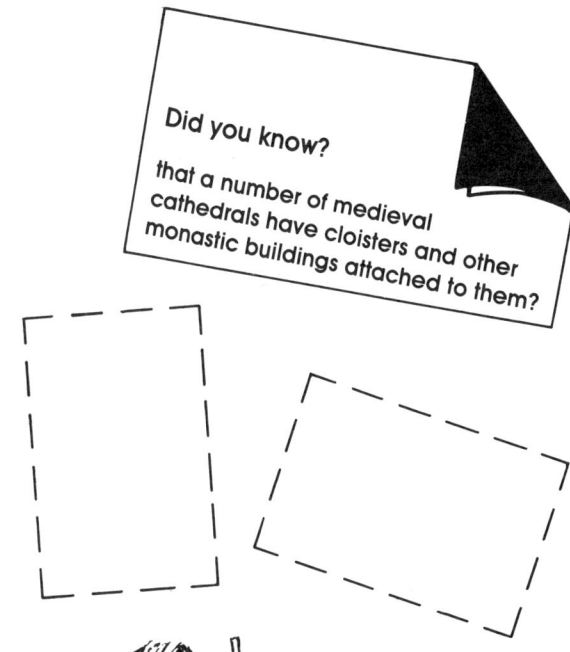

Did you know?

that a number of medieval cathedrals have cloisters and other monastic buildings attached to them?

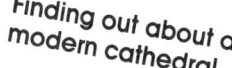

Finding out about a modern cathedral

As you go round the cathedral why not see how the cathedral still plays an important part in the life of the people of the city today. Look at the noticeboards and the posters in the cathedral. What would the city be like without its cathedral?

CATHEDRAL CROSSWORD

Across

1 A man who is a member of the clergy (9)
5 These town roads are to be found outside most cathedral precincts (7)
6 Religious knowledge (2)
8 Sacred promise made by a nun (3)
9 Roman Catholic (2)
12 Three seats – mixed up in SAID ELI (7)

13

(9)

Down

1

(5)

2 Direction in which to look for the altar (4)

3

(9)

4

(5)

7 What you might have to do during the service – when not standing up (5)

You can find the answers on page 24.

10

(5)

11

(4)

WORD SEARCH

In this WORD-SEARCH, twenty-one of the many interesting things you are likely to see on a visit to a cathedral have been hidden. The easiest to find are those which read from LEFT to RIGHT in the normal way – such as CATHEDRAL. Other words read from RIGHT to LEFT; from TOP to BOTTOM; from BOTTOM to TOP; DIAGONALLY DOWN; DIAGONALLY UP. See if you can find all 21 features. (Answers on page 24.)

```
N K C C A T H E D R A L N E O
B K C O L C E D U X F E V A S
R Y R H R S S G W S F A T P S
A D O O S E H O S F N E I T B
S I P P L K K K D P D L P I T
T S E S S L S C O R U E B A B
B L I M T N S E O I S B E N E
C A T H A L M C N N F N E B N
T I T R I P I E A V K R M H C
I R T T N R N R S N W R A E H
P O R S E S T I O V T A O O E
L M W S D L Y P W A I I T O N
U E I C G A T S C L U D R A D
P M Y S L T O S E S S A R B S
U S G W A M M S T C I O E T N
P P I M S E E F H B S F W N K
G E F V S M M O R G A N O H N
F F F A T N I N B I S H T P E
Y G E N O R H T S P O H S I B
```

CATHEDRAL GAME

What you have to do:
(Ask a parent to help you if you get stuck.)
The knight has not paid his dues to the Cathedral. After the service he tries to leave without being caught by the *two bishops.*

You need:
A counter for the knight and two counters for the two bishops – ideally the knight and two bishops from a small chess set.

Rules
1 The knight moves like a knight in chess. He jumps from black to white and from white to black but can only move two squares forward and then one square left or right OR one square forward and two squares left or right.
2 The bishops also move like the bishops in chess – diagonally but only along the black squares.
3 The knight makes the first move from his square in the nave. He tries to land on any one of the four squares marked exit. If he does this he has won the game. The bishops try to stop him. Their squares are marked by mitres.
4 The knight cannot move on to any of the squares already occupied, such as the font or pulpit.
5 Only ONE bishop can be moved at a time. A bishop is not allowed to move on to or across the black squares occupied by the font, tower steps or stairs to the crypt.

Colouring-in
Why not use different paints or crayons to colour-in the playing area to make it easier to play the game?

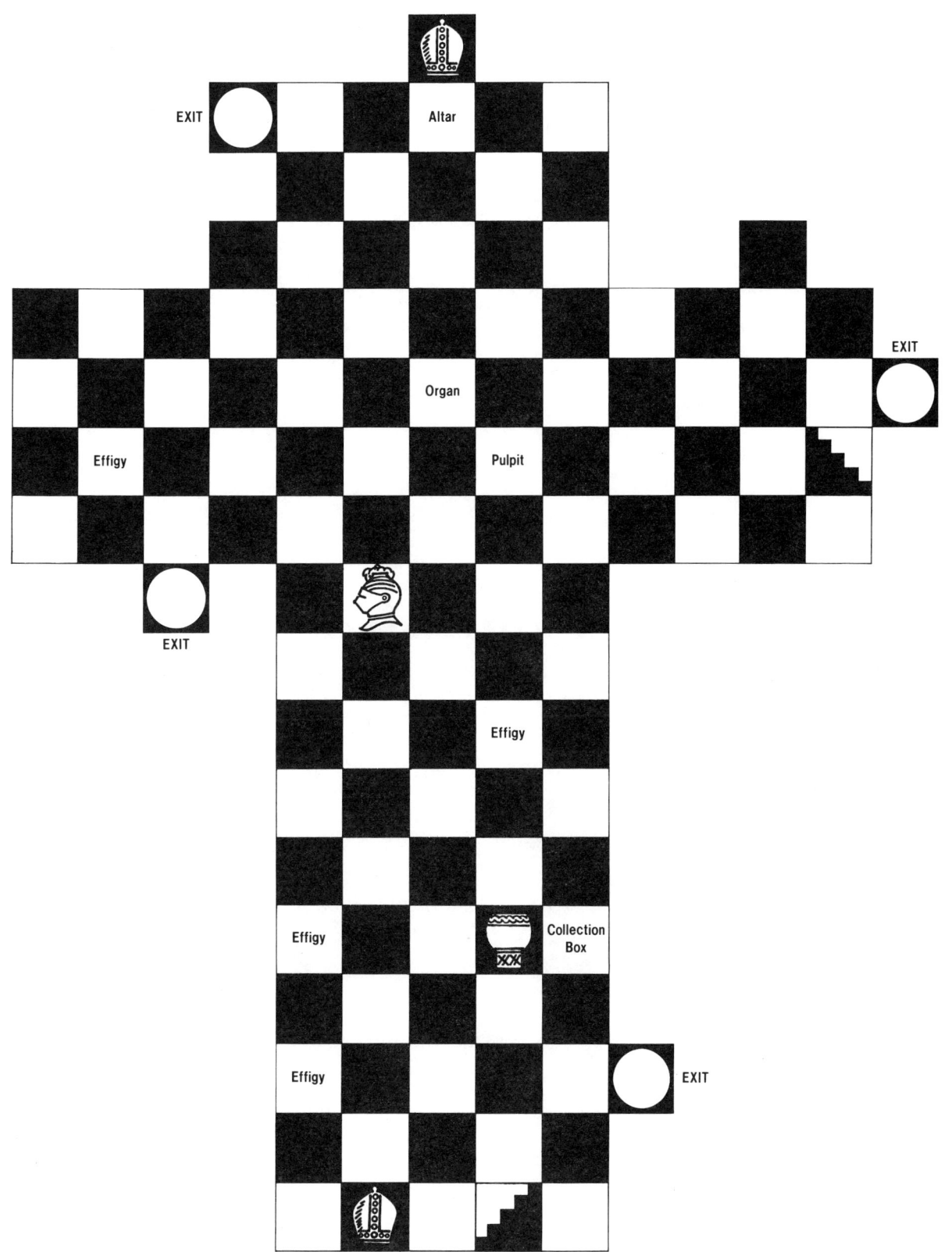

ANSWERS

Crossword

Across

1 Clergyman
5 Streets
6 RK
8 Vow
9 RC
12 Sedilia
13 Cloisters

Down

1 Choir
2 East
3 Gargoyles
4 Altar
7 Kneel
10 Cross
11 Nave

Word Search

Cathedral, Porch, Door knocker, Tower, Spire, Clock, Nave, Pews, Aisles, Font, Pulpit, Brasses, Effigy, Stained glass, Memorials, Transepts, Choir, Organ, Bench ends, Misericorde, Bishop's throne.

SOME CATHEDRALS TO VISIT

BRISTOL (Avon), CANTERBURY (Kent), CARLISLE (Cumbria), CHICHESTER (West Sussex), COVENTRY (Warwickshire), DURHAM, ELY (Cambridgeshire), EXETER (Devon), GLASGOW (Strathclyde), GLOUCESTER, HEREFORD, LICHFIELD (Staffordshire), LINCOLN, LIVERPOOL (Merseyside), LIVERPOOL (R.C.) (Merseyside), LLANDAFF (South Glamorgan), NORWICH (Norfolk), OXFORD, PETERBOROUGH (Cambridgeshire), RIPON (North Yorkshire), ROCHESTER (Kent), ST. ALBANS (Hertfordshire), ST. DAVID'S (Dyfed), ST. PAUL'S (London), SALISBURY (Wiltshire), SOUTHWARK (London), SOUTHWELL (Nottinghamshire), WELLS (Somerset), WESTMINSTER (R.C.) (London), WINCHESTER (Hampshire), WORCESTER, YORK.